INTRODUCING
WORD PROCESSING

CAMILLA BRADLEY

JOHN MURRAY

© Camilla Bradley 1989

First published 1989
by John Murray (Publishers) Ltd
50 Albemarle Street
London W1X 4BD

Cover photograph:
Chris Gilbert

Printed in Great Britain by St Edmundsbury Press

British Library Cataloguing in Publication Data

Bradley, Camilla
  Introducing word processing.
  1. Word processing
  I.   Title
  652'.5

  ISBN 0-7195-4709-1

TASK 100

Recall Task 95 and amend as instructed. When you have finished, proof read carefully, correcting any errors, and print out one copy (in single line spacing).

TASK ~~95~~ 100   (Justify the right-hand margin.)

MEMORANDUM

TO   All Students

FROM   Word Processing Tutor   DATE

I am delighted with the excellent progress you have made over the past few months and hope that this will continue as far as the exam.

So that you can revise effectively, you must go back and make sure that you know all the functions in the WP Operations Checklist. You must also make sure that you remember the Exam Theory. If you have forgotten anything, go back and do it again until you are quite sure you remember it. When you look at both the C— you can test what you know.

~~The next step is to start practising on some past exam papers. This will enable you to get used to the format, length and style of an exam paper. To begin with, you will be rather slow at completing it, but after you have worked your way through one or two, your speed will increase.~~

Your aim is to complete an exam paper in the time specified with complete accuracy. Of course, you will not be able to do this at first – all students have this problem. With practice, you will get better and better, and by the date of your exam, you should be able to manage this. I hope so. Good luck!

CONTENTS

TASK 99

Recall Task 94 and amend as instructed. When completed, proof read carefully and print out one copy in double line spacing with a ragged right-hand margin.

TASK 99

Changes in Education

The office worker is now expected to have a good grounding in Business English and Numeracy and to have had some instruction in Information Processing so as to increase awareness of innovation in the office. The days when a typist was only expected to operate a typewriter are over. There have been widespread c— in e—.

Employers' views are that schools and colleges should train their students to be more aware of innovation in the office, and they have put forward ~~many solutions~~ ideas as to how this can be done. In particular, the E— are keen on training in the workplace.

Change is very necessary, as computers now make it possible to access large amounts of information, and office workers need to be able to analyse ~~and manage~~ this information, and use it for management problem solving and decision making.

The skills required to deal with information ~~in the most efficient manner~~ have now been identified, and apart from teaching Computer Studies, educational institutions are trying to enhance general knowledge.

INTRODUCTION

The purpose of this book is to prepare you for elementary word processing exams. It is assumed that you have a knowledge of the keyboard and that you can set up your word processor ready for operation, and are able to key in work at a reasonable speed.

The theme of information technology runs through the book, and each unit focuses on a different aspect. By the time you have worked through each task and its amendments, you will have read a great deal on this topic, and will, I hope, remember it too!

How to use the book

The book is not intended to be a teach-yourself manual. You will need a tutor to explain how the various functions of your word processor operate, and to help you fill in the word processing operations checklists. The tutor should also explain how you can print out, store your tasks on disc and recall them for later use. Your tutor should also mark your work, and point out any mistakes you have made.

You must work your way through the book systematically, starting at Unit 1. This is because each unit teaches you new points which are carried over into the next unit. If you skip a couple of units, you will find that you have missed some important machine functions or exam points.

WP operations checklist

A word processing operations checklist appears in Part 1 of each unit (for example, see page 5), and they are designed to give you practice on a particular function of your machine. As each word processor has different operating instructions, the checklists set out all the new functions you will be using in each unit.

A space has been left for you to jot down which keys to use to operate the particular functions. If you do not want to write in this book, copy the checklists in a notepad, filling in the details about the keys you must use. Later, you can key in the checklists on your word processor and print out copies for yourself.

The tasks

After the checklist in each unit you will find several keying-in tasks. These have been designed to enable you to practise the functions you have just learnt about. You should work your way through each task, storing them on your disc for use in Part 2 of the unit. You should also print out a copy of each task so that you have a permanent record of your work, and so that your tutor can mark it.

Exam theory checklist

Part 2 of each unit explains some of the theory points which you will have to know in order to pass an exam. These points will be clearly explained, and you will have the opportunity to practise them as you recall your tasks and make alterations to them.

Amendments to text

In Part 2 of each unit, you will be asked to recall each of the tasks you keyed in and stored, and make amendments to them. The amendments will help you to practise the exam points you have been learning about in that particular unit, and will provide good preparation for elementary word processing exams. Finally, you will be asked to print out your work so that your tutor can check it, and so that you have a permanent record of your achievements.

⌐ TASK 98

Recall Task 93 and amend as instructed. When completed, proof read carefully and print out one copy in double line spacing with a ragged right-hand margin.

TASK 9̶3̶/8

THE OFFICIAL VIEW

TRAINING FOR NEW TECHNOLOGY

In the past, people trained for a job once in their lives and expected to keep working at that job until retirement. There was no need for re-training as the pace of change was slow. This has not been true since computers became widely available.

The Confederation of British Industry has long been in favour of training and re-training at any age. Even the Trade Unions have agreed that there should be labour flexibility.

Realising that changes were coming, the Government announced a development programme for schools and colleges. Its aim was to help young people get the skills needed to make the best use of new technology.

Today, traditional skills are rapidly becoming out of date, and the high unemployment levels in some parts of the country have left the field wide open for re-training in the new skills. The G— backed by the C— B— I— has now introduced a whole range of re-training programmes for adults and school leavers.

UNIT 1

1·1 PRODUCING CORRECT COPY – DELETIONS AND INSERTIONS

Before you start any of the keying-in tasks, fill in the WP operations checklist below with the help of your tutor, so that you know exactly how to perform the functions listed. If you do not want to write in this book, copy the checklist into your notepad. Later you can key it in on your word processor, and run off a copy for yourself.

The cursor is the flashing light on your screen which marks your exact position. You need to know how to move it around the screen so that you can put it wherever you want to delete or insert text. When you delete text, you are getting rid of unwanted characters, words or phrases. When you insert text, you are keying in extra characters, words or phrases after a document has been prepared.

⌐WP OPERATIONS CHECKLIST

FUNCTION	HOW TO DO IT
Move cursor	....
Cursor up	....
Cursor down	....
Cursor left	....
Cursor right	....
Delete character/word/paragraph	....
Insert character/word/paragraph	....
Reformat text	....

⟩⟩⟩ SPECIAL POINT   ⟩⟩

Word wrap   This means there is no need to press the return key at the end of each line as the text will 'wraparound' to the next line.

```
Anyone who runs a business will

find a word processor of great

use.  Documents can be prepared

quickly and accurately and

stored for use later on.
```

The words automatically wraparound to the next line at the left-hand margin.

TASK 97

Recall Task 92 and amend as instructed. When completed, proof read carefully and print out one copy with a justified right-hand margin.

TASK 92 7

Unemployment in the Office

Are Secretarial Jobs Safe?

One view of secretarial unemployment rests on the idea that the introduction of word processors will enable firms to cut their labour costs while at the same time raising secretarial 'productivity'.

The theory that office automation will increase the amount of work produced in offices while at the same time reducing the number of staff, has been used as a powerful advertising theme by word processor manufacturers.

On the basis of advertisements and statistics many of Britain's largest and best known companies introduced word processors with the aim of using them to reduce staff and costs.

This does not mean that people were actually sacked, but staff were shed by 'natural wastage', ie any secretary who left the firm was just not replaced. As a result of this, secretarial jobs, which had always been plentiful, started to get more competitive.

Key this in as the last paragraph:

There is still a shortage of secretaries in B— today and w— p— have only slightly eased it. It is true though, that productivity has risen, if you take p— to mean doing more work in the same amount of time.

))) SPECIAL POINT   ))

Using the return key   You only need to press the return key at the end of a paragraph or heading and where you want to leave a clear line space. Most systems show a little symbol or **graphic** on the screen when the return key has been pressed.

```
Do some research first, and

investigate all the popular

brands for sale. ↵

↵

When word processors came on the

market in the late 1960s
```

Press the return key *twice* at the end of a paragraph. If your machine uses **graphics** you can check that they are both there.

TASK 1

Now key in Task 1. When you have finished, check it carefully for errors, store it on disc and print out one copy.

```
TASK 1

If you have ever thought of buying a word processor for use at
home, do not rush out and buy one immediately.  Do some research
first, and investigate all the popular brands for sale.

When word processors came on the market in the late 1960s, they
were large, expensive machines which were only capable of doing
word processing.

This is not the case today, and relatively few machines are
dedicated to word processing alone.  As many shops now stock
them, it is not difficult to go and inspect what is available.

Before you rush out and buy a word processor, examine the reasons
why you want to have one.  Some people feel that this is a way of
getting to know about information technology.

This is fine, if the word processor is capable of running other
programmes.  If, however, it is a dedicated machine, and will do
nothing else but word processing, it will not be sufficiently
versatile.
```

TASK 96

Recall Task 91 and amend as instructed. When completed, proof read carefully and print out one copy with a justified right-hand margin.

TASK 9~~1~~6

UNEMPLOYMENT IN THE OFFICE

THE THREAT TO JOBS

There is no doubt that the capabilities of a word processor – its advanced displays, text editing facilities, large storage capacities and high speed printing – far outstrip the effectiveness of the average typist with an electric or electronic typewriter. Even the Trade Unions which represent office staff have had to admit this.

It is not surprising, therefore, that a large threat has now been posed to the employment prospects of anyone who uses a typewriter to earn a living. **This notion is supported by the T— U—.**

The Government has presented an opposing view of this argument. Their claim is that word processors have been purchased ~~with a view~~ to reducing the shortage of typists which exists in Britain.

The G—

~~They~~ further claim that it is over-simple to conclude, from the studies available, that typing employment could be halved by the mere purchase of word processors.

Word processors introduce the possibility of new areas of work. For example, firms could switch to using more standard documents and more preparatory drafts of the same document.

Moreover w— p— allow firms to produce more work than was ever possible before.

Reformatting   If you have made several corrections to a piece of text, there may be gaps where you deleted a group of words, or you may find that there is no word wrap at the right-hand margin. When this happens, you must reformat, so that the text will return to its original layout. Look at your WP operations checklist (page 5) to see how this is done.

Before reformatting

```
We hope that          you will
accept our offer of
a job and will sign and return
the enclosed contract.
```

After reformatting

```
We hope that you will accept
our offer of a job and will
sign and return the enclosed
contract.
```

TASK 2

Try keying in Task 2. When you have finished, check it carefully for errors, store it on disc and print out one copy.

```
TASK 2

Although word processing systems vary widely, they all have
certain elements in common.

It is a simple task to correct mistakes or make alterations.
You can also move the position of paragraphs or delete them
completely.  This means that many versions of a document can be
quickly and easily produced.  Documents can be stored for later
use, so that if you do not complete your work one day, you can
just continue where you left off the next day.

It is easy to compose text which fits a precise layout or word
length without the bother of printing out trial versions first.
The word processor will give a word or line count, so it is
unnecessary to do this by laboriously counting up the number of
lines keyed in.  The document can be printed out rapidly without
supervision while  new work is being keyed in.  The same document
can also be printed out in different styles or formats, such as
single or double line spacing or italic script.
```

10·2
CONFIRMING FACTS FROM PREVIOUS INFORMATION

Very often, when you are at work, you will be left to check details from previous correspondence or from a reference system. These details may be fairly simple, like names and addresses, or may be more complicated, like times or prices.

You may also be required to do this in the exam, which will mean you either have to look back at the task you are working on or at a previous task in the exam paper to find the information. You will not be expected to invent it, but you will be expected to supply it from previous details. To help you, the first letter of each word will often be given, as in the example below.

EXAM THEORY CHECKLIST

Mrs J Harrison
25 Wood Street
LONDON N21 5LK

Dear Mrs H——

Our current tariff for half board accommodation is as follows:

Single room with private facilities   £45 per night
Twin bedded room with private facilities   £70 per night

As you require a twin bedded room, the cost will be   per night.

Yours sincerely

Key this in as:

(Insert today's date here)

Mrs J Harrison
25 Wood Street
LONDON N21 5LK

Dear Mrs Harrison

Our current tariff for half board accommodation is as follows:

Single room with private facilities   £45 per night
Twin bedded room with private facilities   £70 per night

As you require a twin bedded room, the cost will be £70 per night.

Yours sincerely

))) *SPECIAL POINT*   )))

Proof reading When you have finished keying in work, you must read it through carefully and correct any errors before you store it or print out. The examiner will expect 100% accuracy, so here are the sort of errors to look out for when you proof read.

Keying-in errors You must make sure you have keyed in the correct letters in the correct place.

Wrong   *Right*

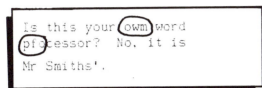

Wrong spacing after punctuation and between words Remember that you must leave:

> one space only between words
> one space only after commas
> two spaces after a full stop at the end of a sentence
> two spaces after any punctuation at the end of a sentence

Wrong   *Right*

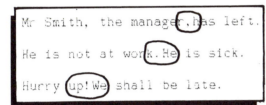   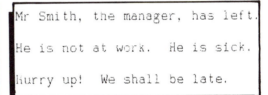

Wrong line spacing There should be one clear line space after a heading.

Wrong   *Right*

There should be one clear line space between paragraphs.

Wrong   *Right*

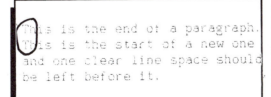

 *TASK 95*

Key in Task 95 with a justified right-hand margin, correcting the deliberate errors which have been circled. When you have finished, proof read carefully, and print out one copy (in single line spacing). Then alter the document to have a ragged right-hand margin, store on disc and print out another copy.

```
TASK 95


                         MEMORANDUM

TO   All Students

FROM   Word Processing Tutor            DATE (Insert today's date)

I am delighted with the excellent progress you have made over
the past few months and hope that this will continues as far
as the exam.

So that you can revise effectively, you must go back and make
sure that you know all the functions in the WP Operations
Checklist.  You must also make sure that you remember the Exam
Theory.  If you have forgotten anything. go back and do it
again until you are quite sure you remembers it.

The next step is to start practising on some past exam papers.
This will enable you to gets used to the format, length and
style of an exam paper.  To begin with, you will be rather
slow at completing it, but after you have worked your way
through one or two, your speed will increase.

Your aim is to complete an exam paper in the time specified
with complete accuracy.  Of course, you will not be able to do
this at first - all student's have this problem.  With
practice, you will get better and better, and by the date of
your exam, you should be able to manage this.  I hope so.
Good luck!
```

TASK 3

Task 3 contains several deliberate mistakes which have all been circled for you, so that you can spot them easily. Make sure you know what sort of errors they are, and correct them as you key in the task. When you have finished, proof read carefully, store on disc and print out one copy.

TASK 3

CHOOSING HARDWARE
The name hardware is given to the physical equipment which forms a computer, or word processing system. Another term often used is configuration.

A typical configiguration consists of a central processing unit, a screen or visual display unit, a keyboard, a disc drive and a printer.

If the hardware is to be used in an office, it will have to withstand long hours of continual use, and the operator should be able to arrange it for maximum comfort.

It would also be sensible to have an integral disc drive, and a printer which can easily be plugged in, or else the office may be crammed with wires.
For home use, the cost of the hardware is usually the major consideration.

TASK 94

Key in Task 94 with a justified right-hand margin using double line spacing, correcting the deliberate errors which have been circled. When you have finished, proof read carefully, and print out one copy. Then alter the document to have a ragged right-hand margin, store on disc and print out another copy (in double line spacing).

TASK 94

Changes in Education

The office worker (are) now expected to have a good grounding in Business English and Numeracy and to have had some instruction in Information Processing so as to increase awareness of innovation in the office. The days when a typist was only expected to operate a typewriter are over.

Employ(er's) views are that schools and colleges should tr(ains) their students to be more aware of innovation in the offi(ce.) and they have put forward many solutions as to how this can be done.

Change (are) very necessary, as computers now make it possible to access large amounts of information, and office workers need to be able to analyse and manage this informati(on;) and use it for management problem solving and decision making.

The skills required to deal with information in the most efficient manner have now been identified, and apart from teaching Computer Studies, educational institutions are trying to enhance general knowledge.

⌐⌐ *TASK 4*

Task 4 contains several deliberate mistakes which have all been circled for you, so that you can spot them easily. Make sure you know what sort of errors they are, and correct them as you key in the task. When you have finished, proof read carefully, store on disc and print out one copy.

TASK 4

(PRI)NTERS

(So) you can choose wisely when you pick a printer(, you) must know something about them.

Basically there are three types available: laser printers, daisy wheel printers and dot matrix printers. You are not likely to choose a laser printer for your own home, as (itis) very expensive because it produces high (gw)ality work within seconds. More probably, you will decide betwee(n) a daisy wheel and a dot matrix. As its name suggests, a daisy wheel printer has a print head like the petals of a da(iz)y, which rotates as it print(s.)(D)ot matrix printers form character(ss) from a pattern of dots. If the dots are spaced (out the) quality of the printed word is not (god.)

TASK 93

Key in Task 93 with a justified right-hand margin using double line spacing, correcting the deliberate errors which have been circled. When you have finished, proof read carefully, and print out one copy. Then alter the document to have a ragged right-hand margin, store on disc and print out another copy (in double line spacing).

TASK 93

THE OFFICIAL VIEW

TRAINING FOR NEW TECHNOLOGY

In the past, people trained for a job once in their lives and expected to keep working at that job until retirement. There were no need for re-training as the pace of change was slow. This has not been true since computers became widely available.

The Confederation of British Industry has long been in favour of training and re-training at any age, Even the Trade Unions have agreed that there should be labour flexibility.

Realising that changes were coming, the Government announced a development programme for schools and colleges. It's aim was to help young people gets the skills needed to make the best use of new technology.

Today, traditional skills is rapidly becoming out of date. and the high unemployment levels in some parts of the country have left the field wide open for re-training in the new skills.

TASK 5

Task 5 contains several deliberate mistakes which have all been circled for you, so that you can spot them easily. Make sure you know what sort of errors they are, and correct them as you key in the task. When you have finished, proof read carefully, store on disc and print out one copy.

TASK 5

(SO)ME POPULAR TERMS

(Tw)o very common terms which crop up in connection with word processing systems (ere) 'stand alone' and (n)etwork'. A stand alone word processor can be used entirely by itself, as it has its own processing unit, screen, disc drive, k(a)yboard and printer.

A network system is one where many word (pl)ocessing screens and keyboards are connected to a central processing unit operating with a (ha)rd disc.

(Th)e hard disc is called a Winchester. It gets its name from the IBM model 3030, which was nicknamed a Winchester after the famous rifle. Hard discs are fix(e)d,(s)ealed units which allow information to be stored and accessed very (fast.

Both) networks and stand alone (si)stems also use floppy discs for storing i(m)formation. Floppy discs are circular sheets of magnetic material which may be enclosed in a hard plastic case for protection.

Errors in punctuation

When the exam day comes; make sure that you arrive in good time, There is no point being hot and flustered, as you have probably got "exam" nerves" already.

Key this in as: When the exam day comes, make sure that you arrive in good time. There is no point being hot and flustered, as you have probably got "exam nerves" already.

Errors in the use of apostrophes

When entering for an exam, its quite likely that each students' aim is to pass. College's pass rates contribute to their popularity.

Key this in as: When entering for an exam, it's quite likely that each student's aim is to pass. Colleges' pass rates contribute to their popularity.

TASK 92

Key in Task 92 with a ragged right-hand margin. When you have finished, proof read carefully and correct any errors. Alter the document to have a justified right-hand margin, store on disc and print out one copy.

TASK 92

Unemployment in the Office

Are Secretarial Jobs Safe?

One view of secretarial unemployment rests on the idea that the introduction of word processors will enable firms to cut their labour costs while at the same time raising secretarial 'productivity'.

The theory that office automation will increase the amount of work produced in offices while at the same time reducing the number of staff, has been used as a powerful advertising theme by word processor manufacturers.

On the basis of advertisements and statistics many of Britain's largest and best known companies introduced word processors with the aim of using them to reduce staff and costs.

This does not mean that people were actually sacked, but staff were shed by 'natural wastage', ie any secretary who left the firm was just not replaced. As a result of this, secretarial jobs, which had always been plentiful, started to get more competitive.

UNIT 1

1·2 COMMON CORRECTION SIGNS

Very often, work that has been produced either in typed or handwritten form has to be amended before the final version can be printed. The amendments are shown by the use of correction signs, and some of the most common correction signs are shown below.

You should have stored all the tasks in Part 1 of this unit, so that you can recall them for use in Part 2, where you have to incorporate the correction signs given below in the exam theory checklist.

┌─ EXAM THEORY CHECKLIST ─────────

CORRECTION	MEANING	INDICATION IN MARGIN (optional)
⌒	Run on with previous paragraph	*Run on*
[or //	Start a new paragraph	NP
⋏	Insert the letter(s) or word(s) written above	⋏
⬭→	Insert the words in the balloon where the arrow is pointing	
firm ~~organization~~	Delete the word(s) crossed out and insert any word(s) written above	♂

⟩⟩⟩ SPECIAL POINTS ⟩⟩

Run on   If a new paragraph is *not* to be used, even though it is shown in the text, this sign is written: ⌒

The words 'run on' may also be put in the margin. This means that you must delete two returns − one at the end of the paragraph you want to run on, and the other which is forming a clear line space before the start of the next paragraph.

Amended paragraph

Correct version

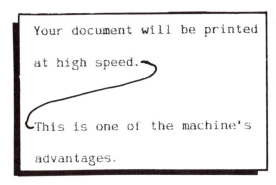

Your document will be printed	Your document will be printed
at high speed.	at high speed. This is one
This is one of the machine's	of the machine's advantages.
advantages.	

TASK 91

Key in Task 91 with a ragged right-hand margin. When you have finished, proof read carefully and correct any errors. Alter the document to have a justified right-hand margin, store on disc and print out one copy.

TASK 91

UNEMPLOYMENT IN THE OFFICE

THE THREAT TO JOBS

There is no doubt that the capabilities of a word processor - its advanced displays, text editing facilities, large storage capacities and high speed printing - far outstrip the effectiveness of the average typist with an electric or electronic typewriter. Even the Trade Unions which represent office staff have had to admit this.

It is not surprising, therefore, that a large threat has now been posed to the employment prospects of anyone who uses a typewriter to earn a living.

The Government has presented an opposing view of this argument. Their claim is that word processors have been purchased with a view to reducing the shortage of typists which exists in Britain.

They further claim that it is over-simple to conclude, from the studies available, that typing employment could be halved by the mere purchase of word processors.

Word processors introduce the possibility of new areas of work. For example, firms could switch to using more standard documents and more preparatory drafts of the same document.

⟩⟩⟩ SPECIAL POINTS   ⟩⟩

In the exam, you may find that some deliberate errors have been made, and you will be expected to correct them. Sometimes the errors are simply ones of keying in, incorrect spacing after punctuation, or using inconsistent line spacing. Errors of this sort were pointed out to you in Unit 1, and you have been trying to spot them and correct them in each task when you proof read your work.

In some exams, other deliberate errors are made for you to correct. These fall into three categories, and examples of each are given below.

Errors of agreement between subject and verb

The problem with sitting an exam (are) that you are nervous and, therefore, likely to makes mistakes. You may overlooks items which have caused you no difficulty in the past.

Key this in as: The problem with sitting an exam is that you are nervous and, therefore, likely to make mistakes. You may overlook items which have caused you no difficulty in the past.

Deletions Words or characters that are not to be typed are crossed out with a single line. The following sign may also be written in the margin to draw attention to this: or

Amended text

I have a ~~very~~ big office.

Correct version

I have a big office.

TASK 6

Recall Task 1 and amend as indicated. When you have finished, proof read carefully correcting any errors, then print out one copy.

TASK **6**

If you have ever thought of buying a word processor ~~for use at home,~~ do not rush out and buy one immediately. Do some research first, and investigate all the popular brands for sale. ⌐

      Run on

When word processors came on the market ~~in the late 1960s~~, they were large, expensive machines which were only capable of doing word processing. ⌐

      Run on

This is not the case today, and relatively few machines are dedicated to word processing alone. As many shops now stock them, it is not difficult to go and inspect what is available.

Before you rush out and buy a word processor, examine the reasons why you want ~~to have~~ one. Some people feel that this is a way of getting to know about information technology. ⌐

      Run on

This is fine, if the word processor is capable of running other programmes. If ~~, however,~~ it is a dedicated machine, and will do nothing else but word processing, it will not be sufficiently versatile.

UNIT 10

10·1
JUSTIFYING TEXT

When a document is printed out, it always has a straight left-hand margin (unless the text is centred or a line has been inset), and the right-hand margin is always ragged. Justifying means giving the text a straight right-hand margin as well. This is done on the word processor by expanding the spaces between words so that all the lines end at the same place.

With some machines, justification can be set in the ruler line or in the information line on the screen. With others it is necessary to call up a special display which allows justification to be selected for the print out. Your tutor will advise you which system your own machine uses.

WP OPERATIONS CHECKLIST

FUNCTION	HOW TO DO IT
Move cursor to ruler/information line or call up special display	....
Set justification (or cancel if justified text is to be printed out with a ragged right-hand margin)	....
Return cursor to screen	....
Reformat document (if it has already been keyed in)	....

New paragraph This is indicated by the sign [or //

NP may also be written in the margin. To do this on your word processor, you must insert **two carriage returns**, one at the end of the old paragraph, and the other at the margin to make a clear line space before the new paragraph begins. Study the following examples.

Amended paragraph   *Correct version*

Anyone can use a word processor.// For this reason, they are very popular.	Anyone can use a word processor. For this reason, they are very popular.

Paragraph deletions Paragraphs or large sections of text to be deleted are usually crossed out with diagonal lines.

Amended text   *Correct version*

A long journey to work can prove to be very stressful. Before accepting a job, find out how long the journey takes.	Before accepting a job, find out how long the journey takes.

TASK 90

Recall Task 85 and amend as shown. On completion, proof read carefully, correct any errors and print out one copy.

TASK ~~85~~ 90

Print out in single line spacing

<u>How to Reach the Outside World</u>

If you want to use your computer as a means of communicating with the outside world, you will need to have access to a phone and you will need some additional equipment to enable you to send and receive information via the phone lines.

Firstly, you will need a serial interface unit that connects to your computer. This will enable your computer to handle information in the standard way used by other manufacturers.

Secondly, you will require a modem. This can be described as a box which will plug into your serial interface at one end, and into the phone socket at the other end. This makes it possible for information to be sent down the phone line.

It should have a cable at least 10' long.

Thirdly, a software package is essential. This will provide your computer with the necessary instructions to enable it to send and receive information.

Of course, you will have to be a subscriber to one of the electronic information services or your financial outlay on new equipment will all be for nothing.

Reaching the outside world is expensive, and you can expect to spend £100 - £200 just to start with.

TASK 7

Recall Task 2 and amend as indicated. When you have finished, proof read carefully correcting any errors, then print out one copy.

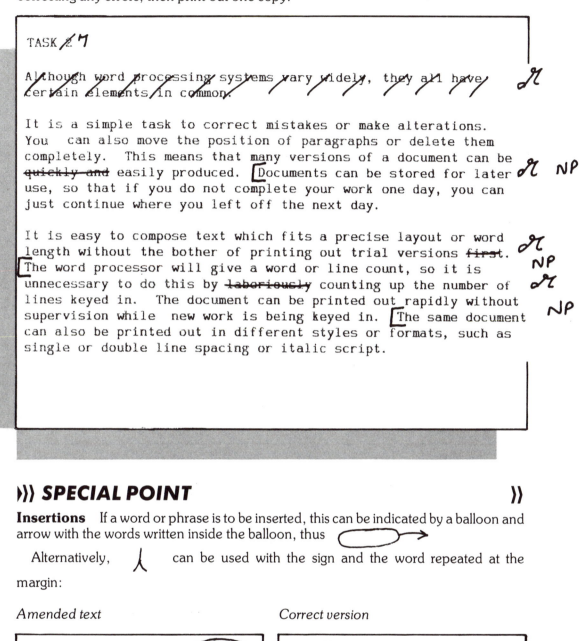

TASK 2 7

Although word processing systems vary widely, they all have certain elements in common.

It is a simple task to correct mistakes or make alterations. You can also move the position of paragraphs or delete them completely. This means that many versions of a document can be ~~quickly and~~ easily produced. [Documents can be stored for later use, so that if you do not complete your work one day, you can just continue where you left off the next day.

It is easy to compose text which fits a precise layout or word length without the bother of printing out trial versions ~~first~~. [The word processor will give a word or line count, so it is unnecessary to do this by ~~laboriously~~ counting up the number of lines keyed in. The document can be printed out rapidly without supervision while new work is being keyed in. [The same document can also be printed out in different styles or formats, such as single or double line spacing or italic script.

)) SPECIAL POINT)))

Insertions   If a word or phrase is to be inserted, this can be indicated by a balloon and arrow with the words written inside the balloon, thus

Alternatively, λ can be used with the sign and the word repeated at the margin:

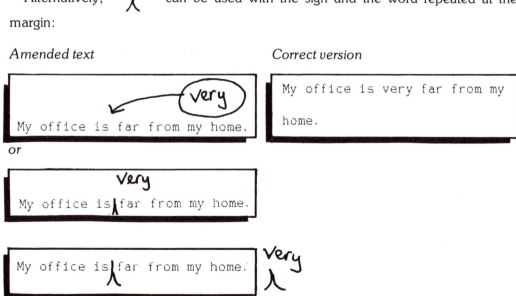

Amended text

My office is far from my home.

Correct version

My office is very far from my home.

or

My office is far from my home.

My office is far from my home.

TASK 89

Recall Task 84 and amend as shown. On completion, proof read carefully, correct any errors and print out one copy.

TASK 8̶4̶/9   *(Print out in double line spacing)*

Bulletin Boards

Bulletin Boards, or BBs, are a means of corresponding with friends or like-minded people via a home computer. They are really clubs for those whose hobby is home computing, and in return for an annual subscription, *which could be as little as £2 or as much as £100,* they enable enthusiasts to get in touch with one another.

User groups or software libraries often run Bulletin Boards of their own, and often have a notices section which is full of computer tips and software which can be copied.

By joining a local computer club, it is possible to find out the phone numbers of different Bulletin Boards, and which ones offer interesting and up-to-date information and which ones do not.

As Bulletin Boards are run by small organisations, they do not have a lot of money to spend, and this restriction means that they have a limited number of incoming telephone lines. As a result it may not be possible to get access except after 1 am. *90% of subscribers check the BBs in the early hours of the morning.*

This can be a truly fascinating hobby, but it can be expensive too. All telephone time will have to be paid for, and this could mean a large telephone bill at the end of the quarter.

Recall Task 24 and amend it as shown. When you have finished, proof read it carefully and print out one copy.

> Address the letter to Miss Jane North 25 Erskine Road LONDON NW4 7ET. Start the letter Dear Miss North and end the letter Yours sincerely Alan Richardson Museum Director.

TASK 2~~4~~9

PROGRAMME OF TALKS

The Technology Museum holds open lectures for the general public on the first Wednesday of the month throughout the year. I should like to call your attention to our Autumn series of talks.

← ——————————— September

Limited

Mr Simmons, the director of Worldwide Computers will be giving a talk on new developments in 'Silicon Valley'. As you probably know, Santa Clara Valley in California was given this nickname in the early 1960s because of the large number of computer companies which set up in business in this area near San Francisco.

← ——————————— October

Professor Fuji from Japan will talk about the ~~commercial~~ uses *A* of the microchip in robotics. He will discuss the new manufacturing processes in which robots are being introduced.

← ——————————— November

A member of one of the new satellite television broadcasting companies will explain the role computers play in satellite ~~broadcasts~~. *A*
communications

TASK 66

Recall Task 61 and amend as indicated. Proof read carefully, correcting any errors, then print out one copy.

TASK 6̶6̶ 6

APPLICATIONS SOFTWARE

Leave 2 clear line spaces

The software packages that are advertised in computer magazines and sold in specialist shops are examples of <u>applications software</u>. They are ready-made programs written to cover certain requirements that a user may have.

Some of these software packages are more suitable for business use and others are for home and recreational purposes. Listed in the columns below are the categories of software that are available for most makes of machine.

<u>BUSINESS USE</u>   <u>HOME USE</u>

Leave 2 clear line spaces

Accounts   Communications
Databases   Educational
Desk Top Publishing   Games
Graphics (Graphs)   Graphics (Art)
Spreadsheets   Programming
Word Processors   Word Processors

Obviously, some of the software listed under home use may be useful if you are running a business. The two categories should be taken only as a general guide.

TASK 30

Recall Task 25, and amend it as shown. When you have finished, proof read it carefully and print out one copy.

> *Address the letter to Mrs P Anderson 94 Wood Street LONDON SW4 4CE. The salutation is Dear Mrs Anderson and the complimentary close is Yours sincerely Alan Richardson Museum Director.*

TASK ~~25~~ **30**

FILM SESSIONS

The Technology Museum holds regular film sessions on Saturday afternoons. Although these are intended for adults, they would also be of interest to teenagers who want to learn something about computers. [The three films to be shown during February are briefly described below.

The History of Computers

This traces the origins of the computer from the first attempts to calculate and deal with complex information, down to the latest developments in the microcomputer.

> *through the most famous inventions in history*

A New Industry

In this, the development of the computer industry is shown. It concentrates mainly on America where the computer industry is flourishing.

Made in Japan

The focus in this new film is purely on the massive Japanese electronics industry which produces much of the equipment used in Europe.

> *It shows how Japan was transformed from a backward nation to a multinational exporter.*

UNIT 7

7·2
LEAVING SPACE OF A SPECIFIED SIZE

In the exam, you may be asked to leave a vertical space within a task. This will either be expressed as a number of clear line spaces, or you may be given a measurement expressed in inches and/or millimetres. You may be asked to leave the space to enhance the layout of the text, or else for some particular reason such as for a picture or illustration or an address.

In order to follow the instruction, you will have to know the **line pitch** of your machine. This may well be displayed with other information on the screen, but if it is not, you will need to know that there are **six lines to an inch** going vertically down the page.

If your machine displays **return graphics** on the screen, it will be easy for you to see that each return graphic keyed in at the margin represents one clear line space.

─EXAM THEORY CHECKLIST─

INSTRUCTION	NUMBER OF LINE SPACES OR RETURN GRAPHICS AT THE MARGIN
Leave 1 clear line space	One clear line space or one return graphic at the margin
Leave 2 clear line spaces	Two clear line spaces or two return graphics at the margin
Leave 13 mm (½ inch)	Three clear line spaces or three return graphics at the margin
Leave 25mm (1 inch)	Six clear line spaces or six return graphics at the margin
Leave 38 mm (1½ inches)	Nine clear line spaces or nine return graphics at the margin
Leave 50 mm (2 inches)	Twelve clear line spaces or twelve return graphics at the margin

UNIT 4

4·1 MAKING ALTERATIONS – MOVING BLOCKS

Keying in text is very time-consuming. If you know how to move the position of blocks of text, you can make rapid alterations to a document. You must know exactly which keys to press, to enable you to define a block of text and remove it temporarily from the screen. You must then be sure that you understand how to replace the text in another position in your document, so that it fits in correctly with the format of the rest of the document. Get your tutor to help you fill in the WP operations checklist below before you start any of the tasks.

WP OPERATIONS CHECKLIST

FUNCTION	HOW TO DO IT
Define block of text to be moved	....
Remove text from screen and put into temporary storage	....
Recall and insert text in its new position	....

⟩⟩ SPECIAL POINTS ⟩⟩

If a whole paragraph is to be moved, the return graphic underneath it should also be moved, so the paragraph can fit correctly into its new position.

Any corrections to the paragraph are better done *before* it is moved, as it is easy to forget them afterwards.

When the text is moved to its new position, it must fit in with the format of the surrounding work.

REMEMBER: if the text forms a new paragraph, it must have a clear line space above and below it.

REMEMBER: if the text runs on from a previous sentence, the full stop at the end of that sentence must be followed by two clear spaces before the text you have moved begins.

When you finish keying in the last paragraph in a task, remember to end with at least two returns, one at the end of the last line of the paragraph and the other at the margin after the last line of the paragraph.

TASK 65

Key in Task 65, setting out the displayed text in three columns as indicated. When you have finished, proof read carefully and correct any errors. Then store on disc and print out one copy.

TASK 65

Dear Customer

In answer to your query about computer games, let me explain that there are three types of games available.

Firstly, there are computer versions of traditional games like Chess, Bridge, Backgammon and Scrabble in which the computer acts as your opponent. Secondly, there are arcade games of the type you would find in your local amusement hall. Thirdly, there are puzzles in which you have to key in text to give your answers or movements. Below is a selection of the most popular games in each category.

TRADITIONAL	ARCADE	PUZZLES
PC Chess	Invaders	Dark Ages
Bridge 2000	East and West	Tower of Babel
Super Scrabble	World War 3	Hades

We also enclose our full list of games software and hope you will find something to suit your interests.

Yours sincerely

Sales Manager

TASK 31

Now key in Task 31. When you have finished, proof read it carefully and correct any errors you find, then move the position of the paragraphs as indicated. When you have done this, store the task on disc and print out one copy.

TASK 31

Software cannot be seen by the naked eye. It consists of instructions which are represented by minute changes inside the processor.

Unfortunately most software is designed only for one type of machine, so you cannot take a disc with information prepared on a particular machine and use it with a different make of machine.

Applications software is the name given to software packages - such as word processing and spreadsheets. The software is designed for a particular machine and often cannot be used with any other machine.

The systems software that comes with your computer is what enables it to operate and run other software packages.

If it did not have software, a computer would not work. When you switched it on, you would merely get a blank screen.

Thank you for your letter to Computer Magazine Problem Page. Many people do not understand what software is because they cannot see it, but I have tried to explain what it is in very simple terms.

⟩⟩⟩ SPECIAL POINT ⟩⟩

When you have moved the position of paragraphs, check to see that you have only one clear line space between them. If you have more space, delete the extra lines. If you do not have one clear line space, put one in by inserting a return.

TASK 64

Key in Task 64, setting out the displayed text in three columns as indicated. When you have finished, proof read carefully and correct any errors. Then store on disc and print out one copy.

TASK 64

Date as postmark

Dear Customer

We are happy to bring to your attention the new graphics
packages we have in stock which will run on your computer.

As you are no doubt aware, there are three types of graphics
package available: art, graph plotting and technical drawing.
We list below the new packages we now stock in each category.

ART   GRAPH PLOTTING   TECHNICAL DRAWING

Master Draw   Plot Plan   Technipad

Micro Art   Digital Graph   Technical Power

Electric Art   Master Graph   Designer

Enclosed is an order form and price list, but do contact us if
you require further information before you order.

Yours sincerely

Manager

TASK 32

Key in Task 32 and proof read it carefully. When you have finished, move the paragraphs as indicated, then store the task on disc and print out one copy.

TASK 32

The moral of this is, that if you wish to buy a computer, you must investigate thoroughly what is available in the brand of your choice.

Though the discs may look the same to the naked eye, the software stored on them is likely to be fundamentally different.

The reason for this problem is partly historical. Competing manufacturers invented their own systems and software to go with them.

The great problem with software is lack of compatability. This means that you cannot take a disc from one machine and use it with a different make of machine.

Not only is there incompatability in software, but even the hardware sold by one manufacturer will differ from that of another.

This led to a lack of standardization in the industry and meant that once you had invested in the products of one manufacturer, it would be very expensive to change over to another manufacturer.

TASK 63

Key in Task 63, setting out the displayed text in three columns as indicated. When you have finished, proof read carefully and correct any errors. Then store on disc and print out one copy.

TASK 63

Databases

The simplest type of database is like a card index filing system. It stores all the items you may have in your address book or in a card index, so that you can look them up easily.

More elaborate databases are programmable, and allow you to analyse the data in the system. This means that you could, for example, work out how much money is owing from your customers, or how many of them live in the London area. Some examples of databases are given below.

Name	Software House	Comments
Alpha File	Comsoft	Good Value
Business Base	Infosoft	Comprehensive
Index Plus	Office Software	Powerful
Pocket Card	Micro World	Easy to Use

Many firms could and do use computerised databases. Estate agents often use them to list their properties for sale so they can deal with requests from house-hunters. Travel agents list the availability of package tours and flights for the holiday-maker. These are but a few examples where databases are used in business.

))) SPECIAL POINT))

When you are keying in any document, remember that you must put Enc at the end, if there is any sort of enclosure mentioned in the draft.

TASK 33

Key in Task 33 and then proof read it carefully. When you have done this, move the paragraphs as indicated and check carefully that you have only one clear line space between each one. Finally, store the task on disc and print out one copy.

TASK 33

Different processors require different operating systems.   For
example, 8-bit processors require different operating systems
from 16-bit processors.

Operating systems vary enormously, and systems designed to deal
with several tasks at once require more complex operating
systems.

MS-DOS

This is the main rival to CP/M.   It was designed by Microsoft Inc
and is a 16-bit operating system originally commissioned by IBM
for use on their Personal Computer.

CP/M

This stands for Control Program for Microprocessors.   It was
invented in the 1970s and is a standard operating system for 8-
bit microcomputers.   More software runs under CP/M than any other
operating system.

In answer to your letter to the Computer Magazine Problem Page,
the computer's operating system enables you to input and output
data, save and retrieve programs and store information on disc.

TASK 62

Key in Task 62, setting out the displayed text in three columns as indicated. When you have finished, proof read carefully and correct any errors. Then store on disc and print out one copy.

TASK 62

Spreadsheets

A spreadsheet is useful for helping businesses or individuals to analyse the financial benefits of a situation or course of action. A spreadsheet is so called because it allows a firm to spread out its accounts on a sheet of paper. It can automatically do any calculations that are necessary, so that the user can immediately see how profitable any decision will be.

Here is a list of some of the most popular spreadsheets available, the name of their Software House and their price.

Name	Software House	Price
Quickcalc	Engsoft	£49
Multicost	New Systems	£70
Pocket Calc	Microstar	£35
First Costing	Datasoft	£59

Spreadsheets can be used for many purposes. For example, a firm could use one to calculate its income and expenditure in order to see if the business was making a profit or not. It could be used to compare the costs of buying equipment or leasing it, or it could be used to forecast the profit on an investment which was being planned. The range of possibilities for spreadsheets is almost limitless.

 **TASK 34**

Key in Task 34 and then move the paragraphs as indicated, checking carefully to see that there is only one clear line space between each paragraph. Proof read your work, store on disc, and print out one copy.

TASK 34

RANDOM ACCESS MEMORY

RAM refers to the short term memory which stores information that is inputted into the computer. This memory can be re-written with new information thousands of times, but the information is lost when the machine is switched off.

A computer has a small internal memory from which information can be quickly retrieved. This internal memory is comprised of RAM or Random Access Memory and ROM or Read Only Memory.

READ ONLY MEMORY

ROM refers to the memory of the machine which is used to store software. It is only possible to use this memory to read the software, and other information cannot be written into it.

RAM is measured in KILOBYTES or K, and 1K is equal to 1024 bytes. One byte only stores a single character of information, so that a computer with 64K of RAM would store less than 30 pages of a book.

Many people are confused about this point, so let me explain it as best I can.

 *TASK 61*

Key in Task 61, setting tabs for the text in columns. When you have finished, proof read your work carefully for errors, store it on disc and print out one copy.

```
TASK 61


                      APPLICATIONS SOFTWARE

The software packages that are advertised in computer
magazines and sold in specialist shops are examples of
applications software.  They are ready-made programs written
to cover certain requirements that a user may have.

Some of these software packages are more suitable for business
use and others are for home and recreational purposes.  Listed
in the columns below are the categories of software that are
available for most makes of machine.

BUSINESS USE                   HOME USE

Accounts                       Communications
Databases                      Educational
Desk Top Publishing            Games
Graphics (Graphs)              Graphics (Art)
Spreadsheets                   Programming
Word Processors                Word Processors

Obviously, some of the software listed under home use may be
useful if you are running a business.  The two categories
should be taken only as a general guide.
```

)))) *SPECIAL POINT*))

It is not necessary to set the tabs at the start of the document. In fact, this is not a good idea if the document is very long, as you may want to change the layout in other ways before you reach the text that is displayed as a table. Set the tabs just before you key in the columns of text.

TASK 35

Key in Task 35, then move the paragraphs as indicated. Proof read carefully, store on disc and print out one copy.

TASK 35

It is very hard for a lay person who is not a computer specialist to understand the difference between BITS and BYTES.

The computer does not deal with each binary number or BIT individually, but groups them together usually into 8 bits.

The word BIT comes from BInary digiT, and it is one of the two digits, 0 and 1, used in the binary number system to operate a computer.

A KILOBYTE or K is equal to 1024 bytes, and 1K represents approximately 150 words. This would be less than half a page of a book.

As many computers deal with 8 bits at a time, a BYTE is generally taken to mean a group of 8 BITS which can be made to store any character fed into the computer. Therefore an 8-bit computer can process information 1 byte at a time.

I hope that my brief explanation will make things clearer for you and get rid of some of the mystique that surrounds these terms.

UNIT 7

7·1
FURTHER DISPLAY WORK –
SETTING AND CLEARING TABS

Those of you who can operate a typewriter know that tab stops are set to enable you to arrange work in columns or tables. The tabs on the word processor are also used to help you align work neatly, and most exam papers will contain some text displayed in this way to test whether you can operate the tab keys properly.

With many makes of word processor, tabs are set and cleared when the cursor is in the **ruler line**. In Unit 5, you learnt to identify the ruler line and the markings on it, and you learnt how to move the cursor into it, and then back on to the screen. Your tutor will advise you if it is necessary, with your make of word processor, to do this again.

You must also be able to identify the special function keys which are used to set and clear the tabs, and you must be able to find the tab key on the keyboard which will move the cursor to any tab positions you have set.

┌─ WP OPERATIONS CHECKLIST ─

FUNCTION	HOW TO DO IT
Move cursor into ruler line	....
Clear old tab settings	....
Move cursor to position of new tab	....
Set new tab	....
Return cursor to screen	....
Identify tab key on keyboard	....
Move cursor to position of tab ready for keying in text	....

))) *SPECIAL POINT*   ))

If the columns have headings, you should leave **one clear line space after the headings**. The text in the columns can be keyed in either in double or single line spacing. This will depend on the instructions you have been given or on the number of items and size of paper. As a general rule, you should follow the style of the draft you are copying from.

UNIT 4

4·2
DEALING WITH SIMPLE ABBREVIATIONS

Very often you will find that you have work which contains abbreviations. A full stop will indicate abbreviated words. You will be expected to know how to spell these words correctly and to enter them in full. Sometimes, when an abbreviation has two meanings, you will have to read the text carefully in order to make the right choice of word.

In correspondence, especially when it is handwritten, it is very common for words to be abbreviated, and you must make sure you recognise these abbreviations and can spell the words correctly in full.

EXAM THEORY CHECKLIST

Abbreviation	Correct spelling	Abbreviation	Correct spelling

DAYS OF THE WEEK

Abbreviation	Correct spelling	Abbreviation	Correct spelling
Mon.	Monday	Fri.	Friday
Tues.	Tuesday	Sat.	Saturday
Wed.	Wednesday	Sun.	Sunday
Thurs.	Thursday		

MONTHS OF THE YEAR

Abbreviation	Correct spelling	Abbreviation	Correct spelling
Jan.	January	Sept.	September
Feb.	February	Oct.	October
Aug.	August	Nov.	November
		Dec.	December

ADDRESSES, SALUTATION AND COMPLIMENTARY CLOSES

Abbreviation	Correct spelling	Abbreviation	Correct spelling
Ave.	Avenue	St.	Street
Cres.	Crescent	Dr.	Dear
Dr.	Drive	Yrs. ffly.	Yours faithfully
Rd.	Road	Yrs. scly.	Yours sincerely

REMEMBER You should not alter abbreviations used in names, such as:
Mr Mrs Miss Ms Dr. Rev. Esq.

or abbreviations of Latin words, such as:
NB etc eg ie et al

or abbreviations of commonly used phrases, such as:
USA UK USSR UNESCO

TASK 60

Recall Task 55 and amend it where shown. Proof read and print out one copy.

TASK ~~55~~ 60

MEMORANDUM

TO   All Sales Assistants

FROM   Store Manager   DATE

COMPILERS AND INTERPRETERS

It has been brought to my notice that you are not clear about
the difference between these two, and cannot explain
adequately to customers the functions that they serve.

> A COMPILER is a program which converts a computer
> program written in Basic or any other language,
> into machine code. It compiles the whole program
> first before running it, and uses the compiled
> version of the program, and not the original, so
> it is impossible to make changes later on.
>
> AN INTERPRETER is a program which checks and
> translates a computer program into machine code
> one statement at a time. It also carries it out
> statement by statement, so that it is easier to
> spot errors.

Inset by a further ½" on each side

You can also advise our customers that if a Compiler is being
used, the program will run very fast. An Interpreter is much
slower, though most microcomputers are supplied with an
Interpreter for Basic.

It is likely that 1 or 2 computer enthusiasts may wish to ask more detailed questions, but from 30 Aug. we will have a direct line to the technical staff at Head Office who can answer further queries.

TASK 36

Recall Task 31 and amend it as shown. Proof read carefully, then print out one copy.

Date the letter 10 Nov. 19-- and address it to Mr J Robertson 21 Langley Cres. NOTTINGHAM NE2 4PR. The salutation is Dr. John.

TASK 3/6

Thank you for your letter to Computer Magazine Problem Page. Many people do not understand what software is because they cannot see it, but I have tried to explain what it is in very simple terms.

Software ~~cannot be seen by the naked eye. It~~ consists of instructions which are represented by minute changes inside the processor.

Run on

If it did not have software, a computer would not work. When you switched it on, you would merely get a blank screen.

Applications software is the name given to software packages - such as word processing and spreadsheets. The software is designed for a particular machine and often cannot be used with any other machine.

The systems software that comes with your computer is what enables it to operate and run other software packages.

Unfortunately most software is designed only for one type of machine, so you cannot take a disc with information prepared on a particular machine and use it with a different make of machine.

End the letter Yours scly. Editor

TASK 59

Recall Task 54 and amend it as shown. Proof read and print out one copy.

TASK 5/9

MEMORANDUM

TO   All Sales Staff

FROM   General Manager   DATE

DISCOUNT SOFTWARE

starting on 28th Dec.,

As a special sales bargain, we are going to cut the price of our programming language software. For the first two weeks of the sales, there will be a reduction in the price of all languages, and for the remaining two weeks, the total reduction will be increased.

Inset the margins by a further 6 spaces on each side.

> Please direct your efforts to selling our current stocks of Cobol, Pascal and Fortran. This is because we shall be stocking new and simplified versions after the sales period.
>
> In the past, sales of Lisp have been slow. Once the current stock has been exhausted, we will no longer be dealing with this language. Try to run down the stock as fast as possible, as it is taking up valuable storage space.

Apart from the usual commission during the sales period, there will be an extra bonus. Details of how this operates are on the attached sheet.

Enc

6 new staff will be joining the company on a temporary basis to help out during the sales. It is expected that at least 2 of them will be taken on permanently from Feb.

⌐ *TASK 37*

Recall Task 32 and amend it as shown. Proof read it carefully and print out one copy.

> Date the letter 2 Dec. 19-- and address it to
> The Rev Baldwin   All Saints Rectory   Park Ave.
> BRISTOL BT2 9SL . The salutation is Dr. Rev Baldwin.
> End the letter Yours scly. Editor.

TASK 3̸2 7

The great problem with software is lack of <u>compatability</u>. This **Caps**
means that you cannot take a disc from one machine and use it
with a different make of machine.

Though the discs may look the same ~~to the naked eye~~, the software *of*
stored on them is likely to be fundamentally different.

Run on

Not only is there incompatability in software, but even the
hardware sold by one manufacturer will differ from that of
another.

The reason for this problem is partly historical. Competing
manufacturers invented their own systems and software to go with
them.

This led to a lack of standardization in the <u>i</u>ndustry and meant   **uc**
that once you had invested in the products of one manufacturer,
it would be very expensive to change over to another
manufacturer.

The moral of this is, that if you wish to buy a computer, you
must investigate thoroughly what is available in the brand of
your choice.

TASK 58

Recall Task 53 and amend it as indicated. Proof read and print out one copy.

TASK 5~~3~~8

<u>Cobol</u>

Cobol is short for Common Business Oriented Language. It was
developed in the USA in 1959 to handle general commercial
programming. It relies on everyday English, rather then on
the use of mathematical terms, so its drawback is that it is
rather lengthy to compose a program, and the program will use
a lot of memory space in the computer. The three main
advantages and disadvantages of Cobol are:

It closely resembles the English language.

A great many programs for specialist use are available.

It has been designed for handling business files.

It uses a lot of memory space.

It is not efficient at carrying out mathematical
calculations.

Writing Cobol programs is a lengthy business.

However, Cobol is now firmly established as a major business
language, and it would be both time-consuming and costly for a
firm which is already using it to try and change its work to a
more modern language.

Inset
the margins
by a further
8 spaces
on each
side.

*Although it came out in nineteen fifty nine, and
has now been overtaken in popularity by Pascal
and C, 7 out of every 10 businesses still use it.*

⌐⌐ *TASK 38*

Recall Task 33 and amend it as shown. Proof read carefully and print out one copy.

> *Date the letter and address it to The Librarian Brentworth College Brent Rd. SOUTHAMPTON SU3 9TN. Insert the salutation Dr. Sir and end the letter Yours ffly. Editor.*

TASK 3̷8

In answer to your letter to the Computer Magazine Problem Page,
the computer's operating system enables you to input and output
data, save and retrieve programs and store information on disc.

Operating systems vary enormously, and systems designed to deal
with several tasks at once require more complex operating
systems.

Different processors require different operating systems. For
example, 8-bit processors require different operating systems
from 16-bit processors.

CP/M

This stands for Control Program for Microprocessors. It was
invented in the 1970s and is a standard operating system for 8-
bit microcomputers. More software runs under CP/M than any other
operating system.

MS-DOS

This is the main rival to CP/M. It was designed by Microsoft Inc
and is a 16-bit operating system originally commissioned by IBM
for use on their Personal Computer.

> *Insert this as the last paragraph:*
>
> *To solve your particular problem, you should ring the manufacturer and ask for a copy of their operating system manual. They also offer a helpline service which is open Mon. to Fri. during office hours.*

TASK 57

Recall Task 52 and amend it as indicated. Proof read and print out one copy.

TASK 5̸7

BASIC

The name of this programming language stands for Beginner's
All Purpose Symbolic Instruction Code. It is an easy
programming language to learn, as it was invented at an
American College to help newcomers learn how to program.

Most computers use some form of BASIC, as it is suitable for
several programming applications. However, many different
versions of BASIC have grown up over the years, and usually a
program just will not run on a computer if the correct version
of BASIC is not being used. The advantages of BASIC are:

> As it was designed for the beginner, there are
> plenty of good text books available to help you to
> learn the language.
>
> There is a lot of cheap BASIC software available,
> so it is not difficult to find the correct
> software for your machine, and you will not have
> to spend too much money to buy it.

Return the inset text to the original margins.

If you want to have a taste of programming, BASIC is the
language to start with. Novices will find that a simple
program can soon be written and run, which will give a greater
understanding of what programming is about.

20 students out of every class of 25 will find BASIC very easy to learn and use. The remaining 5 may have some difficulty, as not everyone can think in the logical way programming demands.

Recall Task 34 and amend it as shown. Proof read carefully and print out one copy.

> *Date the letter and address it to Mr C Smith 29 East Side St. Brooklyn New York USA. Insert a salutation and end the letter Yours sdy. Editor.*

TASK 3/9

Many people are confused about this point, so let me explain it as best I can.

A computer has a small internal memory from which information can be quickly retrieved. This internal memory is comprised of RAM or Random Access Memory and ROM or Read Only Memory.

RANDOM ACCESS MEMORY

RAM refers to the short term memory which stores information that is inputted into the computer. This memory can be re-written with new information thousands of times, but the information is lost when the machine is switched off.

RAM is measured in KILOBYTES or K, and 1K is equal to 1024 bytes. One byte only stores a single character of information, so that a computer with 64K of RAM would store less than 30 pages of a book.

READ ONLY MEMORY

ROM refers to the memory of the machine which is used to store software. It is only possible to use this memory to read the software, and other information cannot be written into it.

TASK 56

Recall Task 51 and amend it as shown. Proof read and print out one copy.

TASK 5̶6̶

PROGRAMMING LANGUAGES

The early computers had to be operated by really skilled technicians. This is because they used binary code, and a typical program had to be written in binary numbers (0s and 1s). This was so difficult that programmers had huge manuals of codes showing them what combinations of binary numbers to use.

By the late 1950s it had become clear that an easier method of programming had to be found, as it was not practical to employ an army of programmers with manuals to work out the machine codes. From the late 1950s, several computer languages were invented which operated with simpler instructions. More languages were brought out in the 1970s.

Return the text to the original left-hand margin of 1½".

FORTRAN (Formula Translation) was brought out in 1956 and ALGOL (Algorithmic Language) in 1958. LISP (List Processing) and COBOL (Common Business Oriented Language) in 1960.

BASIC (Beginner's All Purpose Symbolic Instruction Code) emerged in 1969, as did PASCAL (after the mathematician Blaise Pascal). PROLOG (Programming in Logic) appeared in 1972 and C in 1974.

Return the text to the original right-hand margin of 1".

Most of these programming languages have stood the test of time and are still in use today. Thanks to them, computers are relatively easy machines to use.

It is estimated that by 31 Dec. more than three million people in this country alone will have learnt one of the computer languages, and by 30 June the following year, this number will have increased by one hundred thousand.

Recall Task 35 and amend it as shown. Proof read carefully and print out one copy.

> *Date the letter and address it to Ms V Thomas 41 Fairway Dr. PLYMOUTH PL6 9MT. Insert the salutation Dr. Ms Thomas and end the letter Yours scly. Editor.*

TASK ~~25~~ 40

an ordinary

It is very hard for ~~a lay~~ person who is not a computer specialist to understand the difference between BITS and BYTES. I hope that my brief explanation will make things clearer for you and get rid of some of the mystique that surrounds these terms.

The word BIT comes from BInary digiT, and it is one of the two digits, 0 and 1, used in the binary number system to operate a computer.

The computer does not deal with each binary number or BIT individually, but groups them together usually into 8 bits.

As many computers deal with 8 bits at a time, a BYTE is generally taken to mean a group of 8 BITS which can be made to store any character fed into the computer. Therefore an 8-bit computer can process information 1 byte at a time.

A KILOBYTE or K is equal to 1024 bytes, and 1K represents approximately 150 words. This would be less than half a page of a book.

UNIT 6

6·2 CONSISTENT USE OF WORDS OR FIGURES AND DATES

Numbers appear often in a business document, and should be presented in the same style each time. This also applies to dates. If more than one date appears in a document, they should be keyed in using a consistent style on each occasion. There are no rigid rules governing the treatment of numbers or dates, and if possible you should follow the document style, or that of the organisation in which you work. However, in case there is a mixture of words and figures in the draft you are copying from, some guidelines are given below for exam purposes.

─EXAM THEORY CHECKLIST─

WORDS OR FIGURES   If a sentence begins with a number, key it in as a word, and use words for all numbers throughout the document.

4 new employees will be starting work in the company after the Christmas holiday.	Four new employees will be starting work in the company after the Christmas holiday.

If the numbers in the document are complicated, key in all the numbers as figures.

Out of two hundred and fifty nine employees, thirtynine left the firm last year.	Out of 259 employees, 39 left the firm last year.

DATES   There are many acceptable styles for dating a document. The most popular is probably that which consists of the day, the month and the year, ie 25 March 1989. However, when dates appear in the body of a document, the same style must be used each time.

The goods were sent on 14th April, so they will reach you by 19th April.	The goods were sent on 14 April, so they will reach you by 19 April. or The goods were sent on 14th April, so they will reach you by 19th April.

DATES OF YEARS   It is better to use figures each time, as complicated numbers are involved.

I joined the firm in nineteen eighty nine.	I joined the firm in 1989.

UNIT 5

5·1 LAYOUT OF TEXT – SETTING MARGINS

In this unit you are going to practise setting your own margins on the screen of your word processor so that these margins will be used on the paper fed into your printer.

Ask your tutor to help you fill out the WP operations checklist below and explain what you have to do. Before you can set the margins accurately, you will have to know the print **pitch** you are using – that is, you will have to know how many characters you can print to the inch.

You will also have to know if a **left print offset** is in operation – that is, you must know whether your printing will automatically start a certain number of characters from the left edge of your paper, or whether it will start at the exact position you set your left-hand margin on the screen. With some word processing systems, you do not need to set a left-hand margin on the screen, as the left print offset will act as a left-hand margin when the text is printed out on paper. Your tutor will advise you which system applies to your particular word processor

You will also have to be able to identify the **ruler line** on the screen of your word processor and understand the markings on it. In many systems, the margins are set when the cursor is in the ruler line, so you will probably need to know how to move it into the ruler line and how to return it to the screen.

┌─WP OPERATIONS CHECKLIST─

FUNCTION	HOW TO DO IT
Check pitch	....
Check position of left print offset	....
Move cursor into ruler line	....
Move cursor to position required for left-hand margin	....
Set left-hand margin	....
Move cursor to position required for right-hand margin	....
Set right-hand margin	....
Exit from ruler line and return cursor to screen	....

Key in Task 55, amending the task where indicated. Then proof read, store on disc and print out one copy.

```
TASK 55


MEMORANDUM

TO  All Sales Assistants

FROM  Store Manager                DATE (Insert today's date)

COMPILERS AND INTERPRETERS

It has been brought to my notice that you are not clear about
the difference between these two, and cannot explain
adequately to customers the functions that they serve.

A COMPILER is a program which converts a computer program
written in Basic or any other language, into machine code.  It
compiles the whole program first before running it, and uses
the compiled version of the program, and not the original, so
it is impossible to make changes later on.

AN INTERPRETER is a program which checks and translates a
computer program into machine code one statement at a time.
It also carries it out statement by statement, so that it is
easier to spot errors.

You can also advise our customers that if a Compiler is being
used, the program will run very fast.  An Interpreter is much
slower, though most microcomputers are supplied with an
Interpreter for Basic.
```

Inset by ½" on each side.

TASK 41

Before you key in Task 41, set your left-hand margin at 1½ inches and your right-hand margin at 1 inch. Remember to check your pitch before you start, or your margin settings will be inaccurate. Key in the task with these margin settings. Then proof read it, store on disc and print out one copy.

```
TASK 41

MEMORANDUM

TO The Advertising Executive

FROM  The Research Assistant        DATE  (Insert today's date)

In reply to your queries, the oldest and best known calculating
machine is the ABACUS, which is still used as a ready reckoner
for primitive commercial transactions in the far east.

Another famous invention was the SLIDE RULE which calculated
numbers by using logarithms, and operated by means of a sliding
inserted portion.

Less well-known is the DIFFERENCE ENGINE which was invented in
1850 by the mathematician Charles Babbage.  It was a machine
intended to be used for working out trigonometry tables and
helping to calculate tides.

The last great invention was in the USA when Herman Hollerith
designed a sorting and collating machine which was used to
analyse the results of the US census.  The company he later
formed is now know as IBM, one of the world's biggest and
wealthiest office equipment suppliers.
```

))) SPECIAL POINT))

It is a good idea to develop the habit of setting the margins systematically so that you do not become confused and make a mistake. When you are in the ruler line, *always* set the left-hand margin first and the right-hand margin next. This will prevent you from getting mixed-up and making errors.

Unit 5: Layout of text – setting margins

TASK 54

Key in Task 54, setting new margins where indicated. When you have finished, proof read carefully, store on disc and print out one copy.

```
TASK 54


MEMORANDUM

TO  All Sales Staff

FROM  General Manager                DATE

DISCOUNT SOFTWARE

As a special sales bargain, we are going to cut the price of
our programming language software.  For the first two weeks of
the sales, there will be a reduction in the price of all
languages, and for the remaining two weeks, the total
reduction will be increased.

Please direct your efforts to selling our current stocks of
Cobol, Pascal and Fortran.  This is because we shall be
stocking new and simplified versions after the sales period.

In the past, sales of Lisp have been slow.  Once the current
stock has been exhausted, we will no longer be dealing with
this language.   Try to run down the stock as fast as
possible, as it is taking up valuable storage space.

Apart from the usual commission during the sales period, there
will be an extra bonus.  Details of how this operates are on
the attached sheet.

Enc
```

Inset by 6 spaces on each side.

TASK 42

Before you key in Task 42, check your pitch carefully, then set your left-hand margin at 2 inches and your right-hand margin at 1½ inches. Then key in the task, proof read it carefully and print out one copy, storing the original on disc.

```
TASK 42


MEMORANDUM

TO   The Publicity Manager

FROM   The Research Assistant          DATE (Insert today's date)

Here is the information you require to assist you with your
forthcoming campaign.

The ASCC OR Automatic Sequence-Controlled Calculator was the last
great mechanical invention.  It was eight feet high and fifty
feet long and contained more than a million mechanical parts.

Later inventions were operated by the valve, but little is known
of scientific advances made during the war years, because they
are still a Government secret.

In the immediate post war years, computers were used mainly as
University research machines, and most of the great inventions
were known by their abbreviations.

By 1959, the first commercial computer to be built using
transistors instead of valves was produced by IBM.  The emphasis
had also changed from using the computer as a calculator to using
it as a storage and retrieval system for large amounts of data.
```

⟩⟩⟩ SPECIAL POINT   ⟩⟩

If you forget to set the margins before you start keying in, you can usually just put the cursor at the beginning of your work, enter the ruler line and then set the margins. When you return the cursor to the screen, you will have to **reformat** your work, so that it adjusts to the new margins. See Unit 1 if you have forgotten how to reformat text.

TASK 53

Key in the following task, altering the margins as shown. When you have finished, proof read carefully, making any corrections that are necessary, store on disc and print out one copy.

TASK 53

<u>Cobol</u>

Cobol is short for Common Business Oriented Language. It was developed in the USA in 1959 to handle general commercial programming. It relies on everyday English, rather then on the use of mathematical terms, so its drawback is that it is rather lengthy to compose a program, and the program will use a lot of memory space in the computer. The three main advantages and disadvantages of Cobol are:

It closely resembles the English language.

A great many programs for specialist use are available.

It has been designed for handling business files.

It uses a lot of memory space.

It is not efficient at carrying out mathematical calculations.

Writing Cobol programs is a lengthy business.

Inset the margins by 4 spaces on each side.

However, Cobol is now firmly established as a major business language, and it would be both time-consuming and costly for a firm which is already using it to try and change its work to a more modern language.

TASK 43

Set both margins at 1 inch, then key in the following task. When you have finished, proof read it carefully, correct any errors, store it on disc and print out one copy.

```
TASK 43

MEMORANDUM

TO   The Marketing Manager

FROM   The Research Assistant        DATE  (Insert today's date)

I hope this information will fill you in with the details of
computer development from the 1950s.

By 1958 transistors had been turned into integrated circuits, and
by 1960 they were miniaturised.  Engineers then discovered how to
put thousands of transistors onto a microchip, so that by the mid
1970s, a computer could be manufactured on a chip.

During the 1970s and 1980s there have been many famous brands of
computer which have sold to enthusiasts.  Clive Sinclair's MK14
was probably the first home computer sold in Britain.

The American Commodore PET and Apple II took over both the home
computing and the business computing sectors in the late 1970s.
However, in the early 80s, IBM started to sell its own personal
computer, and immediately took over the business market.
```